REMEMBERING THE CALIFORNIA MISSIONS

A CURRICULUM GUIDE

By Anne Biggs and Kathleen Gorman

Craven Street Books
Fresno, California

Remembering The California Missions: A Curriculum Guide
Copyright © 2013 by Anne Biggs and Kathleen Gorman. All rights reserved.

TO ORDER THIS CURRICULUM GUIDE AND THE BOOK IT IS BASED ON,
PLEASE CALL 800-345-4447

Published by Craven Street Books
An imprint of Linden Publishing
2006 South Mary Street, Fresno, California 93721
(559) 233-6633 / (800) 345-4447
CravenStreetBooks.com

ISBN 978-1-61035-201-7

Craven Street Books and Colophon are trademarks of
Linden Publishing, Inc.

Artwork from the book *Remembering the California Missions* (ISBN 978-1-884995-64-4)
used with the permission of the authors and publisher of that book.

COPYRIGHT NOTICE

All rights reserved. No part of this publication may be reproduced in whole or in part, or stored in a retrieval system, or transmitted in any form or by any means, electronic, mechanical, photocopying, recording, or otherwise, without the written permission of the publisher. CLASSROOM EXCEPTION: Linden Publishing grants teachers who have purchased Remembering the Californian Missions: A Curriculum Guide permission to reproduce from this book those pages intended for use in their classrooms. Reproduction of the material in this book for an entire school, school system, or school district is expressly forbidden.

Contents

About the Authors 4
California and Common Core Standards 5
Introduction 8
Vocabulary—Giving Words Meaning and Giving Meaning to Words   9
Activities for the Missions 11
Pre Post Activities 12

1. El Camino Reál 13
2. Mission San Diego de Alcalá 16
3. Mission San Carlos Borromeo de Carmelo 19
4. Mission San Antonio de Padua 22
5. Mission San Gabriel Archángel 25
6. Mission San Luis Obispo de Tolosa 29
7. Mission San Francisco de Asís (Mission Dolores) 33
8. Mission San Juan Capistrano 37
9. Mission Santa Clara de Asís 41
10. Mission San Buenventura 45
11. Mission Santa Bárbara 48
12. Mission La Purísima Concepción 52
13. Mission Santa Cruz 56
14. Mission Nuestra Señora de la Soledad 60
15. Mission San José 64
16. Mission San Juan Bautista 68
17. Mission San Miguel Arcángel 72
18. Mission San Fernando Rey de España 76
19. Mission San Luis Rey de Francia 79
20. Mission Santa Inés 84
21. Mission San Rafael Arcángel 88
22. Mission San Francisco Solano de Sonoma 92

Directed Reading Comprehension Activity 96
Venn Diagram 97
Triangle Comparison of Missions 98
Comprehension Quiz 99
Review Questions 102
Mission Question Answers 105

About the Authors

Anne Biggs has taught both high school English and Special Education for the last 25 years. She has written RSP curriculum to support Full Inclusion programs for general education teachers in high school and middle school in core curriculum classes. She holds a Secondary English Credential, which she obtained at CSU Fresno, and a Resource Specialist Credential, which she received at Fresno Pacific. In 2006, she was the Northern California Teacher of the Year for California Associated Teachers of English. In 2010, she was a finalist for Special Education Educator of the Year. Her stories and poetry have been professionally published, and she is currently completing a novel, *The Swan Garden*.

Kathleen Gorman is a retired reading intervention and kindergarten teacher. She currently lends support to new teachers who are working towards clearing their teaching credentials. She holds a Bachelor's Degree in Education and a Master's Degree in Reading and Language Arts, along with a Reading Specialist Credential. Her degrees and credential were earned at CSU Fresno. Her professional writing experience includes phonics-based and sight-word-based picture books created for use in her classroom, proposals for educational awards and grants, and professionally published personal memoirs about her family, profession, and friends. She is an active member of the Educational Committee for the Komen Foundation and SCBWI.

California and Common Core Standards

Reading Standards for Literature

Key Ideas and Details

- **RL.4.1.** Refer to details and examples in a text when explaining what the text says explicitly and when drawing inferences from the text.

Craft and Structure

- **RL.4.4.** Determine the meaning of words and phrases as they are used in a text, including those that allude to significant characters

Reading Standards for Informational Text

Key Ideas and Details

- **RL.4.1.** Refer to details and examples in a text when explaining what the text says explicitly and when drawing inferences from the text.
- **RI.4.3.** Explain events, procedures, ideas, or concepts in a historical, scientific, or technical text, including what happened and why, based on specific information in the text.

Craft and Structure

- **RI.4.4.** Determine the meaning of general academic and domain-specific words or phrases in a text relevant to a grade 4 topic or subject area.
- **RI.4.5.** Describe the overall structure (e.g., chronology, comparison, cause/effect, problem/solution) of events, ideas, concepts, or information in a text or part of a text.

Integration of Knowledge and Ideas

- **RI.4.7.** Interpret information presented visually, orally, or quantitatively (e.g., in charts, graphs, diagrams, time lines, animations, or interactive elements on Web pages) and explain how the information contributes to an understanding of the text in which it appears.

Writing Standards

Text Types and Purposes

- **W.4.1.** Write opinion pieces on topics or texts, supporting a point of view with reasons and information
    - Introduce a topic or text clearly, state an opinion, and create an organizational structure

in which related ideas are grouped to support the writer's purpose.
- Provide reasons that are supported by facts and details.
- Link opinion and reasons using words and phrases (e.g., for instance, in order to, in addition).
- Provide a concluding statement or section related to the opinion presented.
- **W.4.2.** Write information/explanatory texts to examine a topic and convey ideas and information clearly.
  - Develop the topic with facts, definitions, concrete details, quotations, or other information and examples related to the topic.
  - Use precise language and domain-specific vocabulary to inform about or explain the topic.
- **W.4.3.** Write narratives to develop real or imagined experiences or events using effective technique, descriptive details, and clear event sequences.
  - Use concrete words and phrases and sensory details to convey experiences and events precisely.
  - Use dialogue and description to develop experiences and events or show the responses of characters to situations.

Research to Build and Present Knowledge

- **W.4.9.** Draw evidence from literary or informational texts to support analysis, reflection, and research.
  - Apply grade 4 reading standard to informational texts (e.g., "Explain how an author uses reasons and evidence to support particular points in a text").

Range of Writing

- **W.4.10.** Write routinely over extended time frames (time for research, reflection, and revision) and shorter time frames (a single sitting or a day or two) for a range of discipline-specific tasks, purposes, and audiences.

Language Standards

Vocabulary Acquisition and Use

- **L.4.4.** Determine or clarify the meaning of unknown and multiple-meaning words and phrases based on Grade 4 reading and content, choosing flexibly from a range of strategies.
  - Use content (e.g., definitions, examples, or restatements, in text) as a clue to the meaning

of a word or phrase.
- **L.4.6.** Acquire and use accurately grade-appropriate general academic and domain-specific words and phrases, including those that signal precise actions, emotions or states of being.

Social Studies

The stories of Junipero Serra, Juan Crespi, Juan Bautista de Anza, and Gaspar de Portola are told as part of this narrative.

Missions, Ranchos, and the Mexican War for Independence

Teachers emphasize the daily lives of the people who occupied the ranchos, missions, presidios, haciendas, and pueblos, using literature, journal writing, and other activities designed to help students analyze carefully selected primary and secondary sources and thus understand and articulate the views of the native population, the Spanish military, and the missionaries.

By analyzing California's geography, students will see how the natural barriers and remoteness of the region influenced settlement patterns during this period.

Introduction

We are retired teachers, who have worked in the California School system for a combination of over 45 years. We know from experience the difficulty in finding quality supplemental material that can be used for all students. While we were teaching, though both at different levels, we worked on curriculum from core material to give our students a better chance at academic success.

Together with our knowledge we feel that we can make your task of teaching easier. We have included vocabulary and comprehension lessons, which continue to be key components to learning. Pre-post activities, along with review guides and a number of additional activities have been added to help diversify the learning process. As the teacher of your class, you have the opportunity to use what matches your students and adjust where needed

Remembering the California Missions: A Curriculum Guide was developed in the hope of making life a little easier for classroom teachers. Fourth grade is the year students learn part of California's history. One of the biggest project-based subjects taught is the history of the California Missions and how these missions played a part in the development of California's rich history. This curriculum guide serves as a secondary supplement to the fourth grade Social Studies text. It supports the Common Core Standards. We created this guide to partner with the historical literature book *Remembering the California Missions*, written by Janice Stevens and illustrated by Pat Hunter. We are thrilled to have the opportunity to work with both Pat and Janice and feel their literature book, along with our guide, are excellent supplements to the fourth grade Social Studies curriculum.

We look forward to creating a series of curriculum guides that can be used in all grade levels and all classrooms. We hope that with the variety of activities we have created, teachers will find strategies to enhance teaching the subject of the California Missions. We also hope you find what you need and have as much pleasure using this guide as we had creating it. We would love to help you continue to enhance your curriculum with more new and exciting guides.

Vocabulary—Giving Words Meaning and Giving Meaning to Words

This strategy was created to help teachers familiarize students with vocabulary words in a given book or unit taught. These steps are a guide for teachers to use to help their students make sense of the words they come across in reading.

There are six steps taught when using this method.

Step 1—Introduce the word to the class by:

   a) Writing the word on the whiteboard

   b) Reading the word to the class

   c) Asking students to repeat the word back to you

   d) Example: "The word is *adobe*. What's the word? Class responds, "The word is *adobe*."

Step 2—Present a student-friendly explanation.

   e) Teacher states the word, then tells the class the definition.

   a) Example: "*Adobe* means sun-dried bricks made from clay and straw."

   b) Students repeat the explanation of the word.

   c) When possible the teacher should also show a picture of the word (for any ELL this is a good visual).

Step 3—Reprase the explanation, asking students to complete the statement by substituting the new word.

   a) Teacher reads a sentence and students supply the new word.

   b) Example: "The Indians used *adobe* to create strong walls when building their homes."

Step 4—Provide examples or a sentence to illustrate the word.

   a) Teacher reads the new sentence.

   b) Example: "One of the common materials used in the construction of the missions was *adobe* bricks."

Step 5—Check for understanding

Option 1: Ask deep processing questions.

Option 2: Check understanding using examples and non-examples.

If this is an example of adobe, put thumbs up; if not thumbs down.

Adobe

    a) a type of wheat

    b) a dried brick

Step 6—If appropriate, have students generate their own examples.

    a) Example: "Tell your partner where you might find adobe buildings."

    b) Example: "Tell your partner how adobe was made."

    c) Example: "Draw a picture of what an adobe brick building might look like."

Activities for the Missions

- Show a map of California, and ask students to identify where they live, and then where they think the missions might be in relation to their home.

- Prompt students to name the missions.

- Journal entry: Anything you know or have learned about the missions. (At least 5 sentences. If you know nothing, include why you don't know anything.)

- In 1542, when Juan Rodriquez Cabrillo first visited the barren countryside we now know as San Diego, what do you think he saw?

- Draw a picture of what you think San Diego may have looked like in 1542. Add the color and detail you think Cabrillo might have seen.

- Write a journal entry of 5-10 sentences about he might have felt when he realized that the country was so barren.

- Create a timeline of the Spanish government pursuing an area to establish the missions.

- Create a profile of one of the characters who was the most responsible for the development of the missions, such as Juan Rodriguez Cabrillo, Sebastian Vizaino, Gaspar de Portola, Father Junipero Serra.

- Detail the two expeditions by sea that were made to California before 1769.

- Write a reflection of at least 10 sentences on what you learned about the missions.

- Discuss markers that you have seen while traveling around and explain why you think you remember it more than others you have seen.

- Design a street marker that you would want to identify something special to you. Share your marker and explain why it was important.

- Research El Camino Reál and write two descriptive paragraphs. Use a resource other than this literature book.

- Write a letter to the *Los Angeles Times* (10 sentences) to explain why the staff bells should be placed along the high way.

- Write two paragraphs explaining what local famous buildings or sites should have markers to identify them (i.e. schools, universities, churches)

- Complete a 10-sentence journal describing what you have learned in a chapter assigned by your teacher. Include why it was important.

- If you were building a mission, make a list of what you think you would need to make it successful.

- Write a letter explaining why you think the Carmel Mission should become the first cathedral in California.

- Write a journal entry explaining what you think the land looked like in California when the missions were being built.

- Pick one mission and create a timeline of its destruction and reconstruction.

- Create a brief history of those people who were instrumental in the reconstruction of the mission you picked.

Pre Post Activities

Teachers, here are some suggestions for pre and post activities for your class. Pick and choose what fits best for you.

Pre-
1. Whole class: Create a KWL chart.
2. Students: On a map of California, plot and label each mission.

Ongoing-
1. Be Father Serra's right-hand person and keep a journal of your trip along the El Camino Reál.
2. Put yourself in the shoes of the neophytes. What would your life be like in a given mission on a day to day basis?
3. Create a timeline of the Spanish government pursuing an area to establish the missions. (Timeline of dedication of each mission.)
4. If you were a trader and wanted to trade with the missions, make a list of what you think the missionaries might have traded with you.

Post-
1. Pick two missions (student's choice) and fill in the Venn Diagram comparing and contrasting the missions.
2. Design a bell that might hang in a mission.
3. Design a street marker that could identify something special to you. Share your marker with your class and explain why you chose the design and its importance to you.
4. Pretend you are a missionary and write a letter of thanks to either President Buchanan or President Lincoln for their support.
5. Pick a mission and create a pamphlet with detailed information to encourage visitors to come to your mission.
6. Create an eye catching poster announcing your chosen mission to the class.
7. Play Missions Jeopardy with your class. (guide included)

1. El Camino Reál

- King's Highway
- 1769–1906
- 700 Miles
- Mustard Seed
- Father Junipero Serra
- Mrs. Forbes
- Native Daughters of the Golden West

VOCABULARY

1. ALLUVIAL (muddy, sandy, grainy)
2. ACCOMMODATE (allow, provide, permit)
3. PROPOSAL (plan, offer, suggestion)
4. DIVERGING (wandering, departing, moving away)
5. NEOPHYTE (convert, beginner, trainee)
6. MOMENTOUS (important, meaningful, significant)
7. COMMEMORATE (honor, remember, observe)

EL CAMINO REÁL

Create your own sentences below showing you understand the meaning of each vocabulary word.

1. ALLUVIAL (muddy, sandy, grainy)
The **alluvial** plains of California were often difficult for travelers on their expeditions.

2. ACCOMMODATE (allow, provide, permit)
The roads had to be widened to **accommodate** people going in the other direction.

3. PROPOSAL (plan, offer, suggestion)
The **proposal** offered by the Indians was accepted by the missionaries.

4. DIVERGING (wandering, departing, moving away)
The Indians were **diverging** from the missions because of the raids.

5. NEOPHYTE (convert, beginner, trainee)
The **neophyte** Indians were willing to do anything to stay at the missions.

6. MOMENTOUS (important, meaningful, significant)
It was a **momentous** occasion when the children came to view the mission for the first time.

7. COMMEMORATE (honor, remember, observe)
People would **commemorate** the special days of the mission for a long time to come.

EL CAMINO REÁL

Answer each question below in a complete sentence.

1. What was another name for the "El Camino Reál?"

_____

_____

2. How far did El Camino Reál extend?

_____

_____

3. Mustard seed was first used as markers. What type of identifying markers were used next?

_____

_____

4. Who chose the mission bell on a walking stick to become the new permanent marker to identify the roadway for the missions?

_____

_____

5. How was the last mission identified in 1963, marking the end of the El Camino Reál?

_____

_____

2. Mission San Diego de Alcalá

- 1774
- Attacked by Neophytes
- Father Jayme
- Earthquakes
- Later Sold as Private Property
- 1862 Returned to the Catholic Church

VOCABULARY

1. AMBITIOUS (determined, motivated, aspiring)
2. ADJACENT (nearby, adjoining, closest)
3. INADEQUATE (scarce, insufficient, scant)
4. CONSTRUCTED (built, created, assembled)
5. DELIBERATELY (on purpose, thoughtfully, carefully)
6. DIVERGING (wandering, swerving, departing)

Create your own sentences below showing you understand the meaning of each vocabulary word.

1. AMBITIOUS (determined, motivated, aspiring)
Because of Father Serra's **ambitious** plans, the missions have become landmarks in California.

2. ADJACENT (nearby, adjoining, closest)
The main building of the mission was **adjacent** to the church.

3. INADEQUATE (scarce, insufficient, scant)
There was an **inadequate** amount of food to feed all the Indians.

4. CONSTRUCTED (built, created, assembled)
The new cathedral was **constructed** after the mission was completed.

5. DELIBERATELY (on purpose, thoughtfully, carefully)
The missionaries **deliberately** brought all the Indians to live in the mission.

6. DIVERGING (wandering, swerving, departing)
The sign pointed to a road **diverging** from the highway that led to the mission.

Mission San Diego de Alcalá

Answer each question below in a complete sentence.

1. Which mission is considered the mother of the California missions?

_____

_____

2. Why do you think it was given this name?

_____

_____

3. Describe what happened to Mission San Diego de Alcalá.

_____

_____

4. Why were the missionaries not able to save the land?

_____

_____

5. Explain why Mission San Diego de Alcalá had to be rebuilt three times.

_____

_____

3. Mission San Carlos Borromeo de Carmelo

- June 3, 1770
- Moved to Carmel Due to Lack of Water
- Father Serra's Bible (first library in California)

VOCABULARY

1. ACCESSIBLE (available, nearby, reachable)
2. EVANGALIZE (convert, persuade, convince)
3. OCCURRENCE (event, incident, occasion)
4. SANCTUARY (reserve, shelter, protection)
5. CONFISCATED (seized, taken, removed)
6. RESTORATION (repair, rebuild, restore)
7. CONTINUOUS (ongoing, endless, nonstop)

Mission San Carlos Borromeo de Carmelo

Create your own sentences below showing you understand the meaning of each vocabulary word.

1. ACCESSIBLE (available, nearby, reachable)
The crops were not **accessible** to the Indians after the storm.

2. EVANGALIZE (convert, persuade, convince)
The priests tried to **evangelize** the Indians as they came to the missions for food.

3. OCCURRENCE (event, incident, occasion)
There was one **occurrence** when the missions were attacked by wild Indians and the supplies were stolen.

4. SANCTUARY (reserve, shelter, protection)
The missions were a **sanctuary** when severe storms came during the winter.

5. CONFISCATED (seized, taken, removed)
All their belongings were **confiscated** when the churches were raided by the rebels.

6. RESTORATION (repair, rebuild, restore)
The Indian workers completed a **restoration** of the mission after the earthquakes.

7. CONTINUOUS (ongoing, endless, nonstop)
The chapel has been in **continuous** use for two centuries.

MISSION SAN CARLOS BORROMEO DE CARMELO

Answer each question below in a complete sentence.

1. When was this mission formally established?

2. This was another mission that had to be relocated. Why?

3. Describe how Father Serra lived.

4. When did Father Serra die?

5. Where was Father Serra's body laid to rest?

6. Who rescued the Mission San Carlos Borromeo de Carmelo in 1931 from being totally destroyed?

7. The chapel at this mission enjoys what distinction?

4. Mission San Antonio de Padua

- July 14, 1771
- Appearance of Single Indian Woman
- Labor Provided by Salinan Indians
- Earthquake, 1906
- Joseph R. Knowland Influenced Restoration

VOCABULARY

1. PROXIMITY (near, close, vicinity)
2. PROSPEROUS (wealthy, booming, thriving)
3. EXPOSURE (contact, publicity, spotlight)
4. DETERIORATION (decline, worsening, corrosion)
5. RECRUIT (trainee, newcomer, rookie)

Create your own sentences below showing you understand the meaning of each vocabulary word.

1. PROXIMITY (near, close, vicinity)
The fields where in close **proximity** to the mission.

2. PROSPEROUS (wealthy, booming, thriving)
The missions became **prosperous** when the Indians were able to sell their products.

3. EXPOSURE (contact, publicity, spotlight)
The crops suffered from too much **exposure** to the heat and dried up before the harvest.

4. DETERIORATION (decline, worsening, corrosion)
The **deterioration** of the churches caused many people to abandon the missions.

5. RECRUIT (trainee, newcomer, rookie)
Indian **recruits** were welcomed into the missions by the priests.

Mission San Antonio de Padua

Answer each question below in a complete sentence.

1. When was Mission San Antonio de Padua founded?

_____

2. Why do you think Father Serra felt so good about selecting this spot for a mission?

_____

_____

3. Who provided the labor for the construction of the mission compound?

_____

_____

4. List some events that occurred which caused the deterioration of Mission San Antonio de Padua.

_____

_____

5. Why do you think Abraham Lincoln decreed the mission be returned to the hierarchy of the Catholic Church?

_____

_____

6. Who was influential in the restoration of this mission?

_____

_____

7. What happened in 1906 that caused more problems with the restoration of the mission?

_____

_____

8. Why is the statue of Saint Anthony important to this mission?

_____

_____

5. Mission San Gabriel Archángel

- September 8, 1771
- Tongva Indian
- Was Rebuilt Due to Flooding
- Joseph (Juan Jose) Chapman, Once Considered a Pirate, Was a Craftsman in Ship Building

VOCABULARY

1. CONVERTED (changed, renewed, improved)
2. ABUNDANT (lavish, plentiful, rich)
3. PRESERVED (conserved, saved, unspoiled)
4. RECOMMENDATION (approval, blessing, sanction)
5. HOSPITALITY (welcome, warmth, kindness)
6. EPIDEMICS (plagues, outbreaks, eruptions)
7. AMNESTY (pardon, forgiveness, absolution)

MISSION SAN GABRIEL ARCHÁNGEL

Create your own sentences below showing you understand the meaning of each vocabulary word.

1. CONVERTED (changed, renewed, improved)
At the missions, priests **converted** many Indians to the teachings of the Bible at the missions.

2. ABUNDANT (lavish, plentiful, rich)
Supplies were **abundant** after the crops were harvested at the mission.

3. PRESERVED (conserved, saved, unspoiled)
The bishop's goal was to **preserve** the mission close to its original state before the earthquake.

4. RECOMMENDATION (approval, blessing, sanction)
The **recommendations** for changes to the mission were approved by the priests.

5. HOSPITALITY (welcome, warmth, kindness)
The missions provided **hospitality** to travelers who needed help during hard times.

6. EPIDEMICS (plagues, outbreaks, eruptions)
Parents were concerned that the **severe** epidemics would kill their children.

7. AMNESTY (pardon, forgiveness, absolution)
The mission provided **amnesty** to the Indians if they worked hard and went to mass.

Answer each question below in a complete sentence.

1. Do you believe the legend about what brought peace between the Tongva Indians and the Fathers?

2. What caused the goodwill that was established between the Indians and the Fathers to be destroyed?

3. Mission San Gabriel Archángel was built two times. Explain why and describe the materials used to build and rebuild it.

4. Where did the copper baptismal font and silver baptismal shell come from?

5. Explain why this mission was called the "Pride of all Missions."

6. Which government confiscated the mission properties?

7. How did President James Buchanan help the mission?

8. Why do you think it was necessary to construct the asistencia (sub-mission outpost) to Mission San Gabriel?

_____

_____

9. What do you find most interesting about Joseph (Juan José) Chapman?

_____

_____

6. Mission San Luis Obispo de Tolosa

- September 1, 1772
- Chumash Indians
- 2nd Construction Due to Fire Set by Indians
- Father John Harnett
- The Bears

VOCABULARY

1. ADMINISTRATOR (manager, supervisor, director)
2. PREVALENT (common, frequently, often)
3. PRIMITIVE (basic, simple, coarse)
4. TRADITIONAL (old-fashioned, conventional, customary)
5. SUPERVISION (direction, control, guidance)
6. REPUTATION (character, standing, status)
7. ACCOMMODATE (lodge, adjust, adapt)
8. CRITICISM (disapproval, reproach, blame)
9. AMBITIOUS (determined, aspiring, motivated)
10. ADJACENT (next-to, nearby, adjoining)

MISSION SAN LUIS OBISPO DE TOLOSA

Create your own sentences below showing you understand the meaning of each vocabulary word.

1. ADMINISTRATOR (manager, supervisor, director)
The **administrator** would make the final decisions about any changes.

2. PREVALENT (common, frequently, often)
A **prevalent** custom was for the Indians to come and spend the night at the missions.

3. PRIMITIVE (basic, simple, coarse)
The missionaries often thought the Indians were too **primitive** to be baptized.

4. TRADITIONAL (old-fashioned, conventional, customary)
Over the years, the **traditional** churches were changed to adapt to the environment.

5. SUPERVISION (direction, control, guidance)
The missionaries provided **supervision** to help the Indians learn skills.

6. REPUTATION (character, standing, status)
The missions had a legendary **reputation** of never turning anyone away.

7. ACCOMMODATE (lodge, adjust, adapt)
The missionaries tried to **accommodate** the Indians during winter months.

_____

_____

8. CRITICISM (disapproval, reproach, blame)
There was a lot of **criticism** by the government of the missions.

_____

_____

9. AMBITIOUS (determined, aspiring, motivated)
The restoration was considered an **ambitious** project for the missionaries.

_____

_____

10. ADJACENT (next-to, nearby, adjoining)
The statues were **adjacent** to the chamber's large doors.

_____

_____

Mission San Luis Obispo de Tolosa

Answer each question below in a complete sentence.

1. Who helped the missionaries construct the original buildings? What materials did they use?

_____

_____

2. Why do you think they were willing to help the missionaries?

_____

_____

3. Why did a second mission need to be constructed?

_____

_____

4. List some of the items produced by this mission when it was prosperous.

_____

_____

5. Why did Father John Harnett want to tear down the modernization work done on the mission?

_____

_____

6. Do you think this was a wise decision? Why or why not?

_____

_____

7. How was Santa Margarita Asistencia similar to Mission San Luis Obispo?

_____

_____

7. Mission San Francisco de Asís (Mission Dolores)

- **June 29, 1776**
- **Mission Dolores**
- **St. Francis Asís**
- **Measles Epidemic**
- **Gold Rush**
- **Earthquake and Fires**

VOCABULARY

1. SUBSEQUENT (successive, following, later)
2. LAUNCHED (leaped, started, began)
3. INADEQUATE (scant, scarce, lacking)
4. COMMERCIAL (profitable, trade, mercantile)
5. CONFISCATED (seized, stolen, impounded)
6. ENSUING (following, arising, developing)
7. DEMOLISHED (destroyed, ruined, wrecked)
8. PREDOMINATE (prevail, lead, dominate)

7. Mission San Francisco de Asís (Mission Dolores)

Create your own sentences below showing you understand the meaning of each vocabulary word.

1. SUBSEQUENT (successive, following, later)
Subsequent visits by new priests brought fresh ideas to the missions.

2. LAUNCHED (leaped, started, began)
The missionaries **launched** campaigns to restore the missions.

3. INADEQUATE (scant, scarce, lacking)
During the winter months, supplies were often **inadequate** for the missions.

4. COMMERCIAL (profitable, trade, mercantile)
Traders brought many **commercial** items to the priests at the missions.

5. CONFISCATED (seized, stolen, impounded)
Indians **confiscated** some of the crops to feed their families.

6. ENSUING (following, arising, developing)
After its construction, the Mission Dolores chapel survived **ensuing** disasters, such as the 1906 earthquake.

7. DEMOLISHED (destroyed, ruined, wrecked)
The Fathers would sometimes **demolish** buildings in the missions so they could restore them to their natural beauty.

_____

_____

8. PREDOMINATE (prevail, lead, dominate)
The large churches often **predominate** the other buildings at the missions.

_____

_____

7. Mission San Francisco de Asís (Mission Dolores)

Answer each question below in a complete sentence.

1. Do you think the San Francisco Bay could really accommodate all the ships in Spain? Why or why not?

_____

_____

2. This mission is named in honor of whom?

_____

_____

3. Who came to help the Fathers with the construction of the mission and its buildings?

_____

_____

4. What caused the Indians to flee the mission?

_____

_____

5. How did the Mexican War of Independence affect Mission Dolores?

_____

_____

6. Describe what happened to the missions when the Gold Rush struck.

_____

_____

7. Why do you think Mission Dolores's chapel survived an earthquake and fire when all the surrounding buildings did not?

_____

_____

8. Mission San Juan Capistrano

- November 1, 1776
- Fathers de Lasuén and Amurrio
- The Bells
- The Swallows
- Earthquake
- Serra Chapel

VOCABULARY

1. LEGENDARY (renowned, famous, well-known)
2. INSCRIBED (engraved, carved, etched)
3. QUELL (crush, defeat, subdue)
4. TURMOIL (chaos, confusion, havoc)
5. ORNAMENTAL (showy, decorated, ornate)
6. REENACTMENT (rebuild, demonstrate, recreate)
7. ILLUSTRATE (explain, prove, show)

Mission San Juan Capistrano

Create your own sentences below showing you understand the meaning of each vocabulary word.

1. LEGENDARY (renowned, famous, well-known)
Over time, the missions gained near-**legendary** status in the state of California.

_____

_____

2. INSCRIBED (engraved, carved, etched)
Saints' names were often **inscribed** on the statues at the missions.

_____

_____

3. QUELL (crush, defeat, subdue)
It was important to **quell** any conflicts between the Spanish and the Indians.

_____

_____

4. TURMOIL (chaos, confusion, havoc)
There was a lot of **turmoil** between the Spanish and California's officials.

_____

_____

5. ORNAMENTAL (showy, decorated, ornate)
The **ornamental** designs of the mission were widely admired.

_____

_____

6. REENACTMENT (rebuild, demonstrate, recreate)
The **reenactment** of historical occurrences are major events at the missions.

_____

_____

7. ILLUSTRATE (explain, prove, show)
Painters would often **illustrate** the beauty of the missions in their paintings.

_____

_____

Mission San Juan Capistrano

Answer each question below in a complete sentence.

1. What legend is celebrated every year at this mission?

2. Why was it necessary for Fathers de Lasuén and Amurrio to wait in San Diego before making the trip to San Juan Capistrano to set up the founding of this newest mission?

3. Why do you think the soldiers buried the bells?

4. What happened on November 1, 1776?

5. How would the missionaries benefit from teaching the Indians the skills of weaving, carpentry, and agriculture?

6. List the materials used in the building of the church.

7. Several devastating events happened to Mission San Juan Capistrano. List three of these events.

8. What is the historical significance of the Serra Chapel?

_____

_____

9. Three cultures—American Indians, Spaniards, and Mexican ranchos—are represented at the mission. Which do you think had the strongest influence and why?

_____

_____

9. Mission Santa Clara de Asís

- **January 12, 1777**
- **Flooding**
- **Father Peña**
- **Jesuit Order**
- **Santa Clara College**

VOCABULARY

1. AUTHORIZED (lawful, approved, certified)
2. IMPOSING (striking, grand, burdensome)
3. SUPERVISED (managed, directed, observed)
4. FRAILTY (sick, weakness, delicate)
5. CONFRONTATIONS (conflict, battle, fight)
6. PROSPERITY (wealthy, success, affluent)
7. REMNANTS (leftovers, pieces, fragments)
8. ENDURANCE (strength, stamina, persistence)

Mission Santa Clara de Asís

Create your own sentences below showing you understand the meaning of each vocabulary word.

1. AUTHORIZED (lawful, approved, certified)
California's government was **authorized** to control the trade going on at the missions.

2. IMPOSING (striking, grand, burdensome)
The Spanish soldiers put **imposing** restrictions on the mission priests.

3. SUPERVISED (managed, directed, observed)
In the beginning, many of the Indians had to be **supervised** by the priests.

4. FRAILTY (sick, weakness, delicate)
Father Serra's **frailty** forced him to cut back on his work.

5. CONFRONTATIONS (conflict, battle fight)
There were many **confrontations** between the soldiers and the priests.

6. PROSPERITY (wealthy, success, affluent)
After developing trade skills, the missions enjoyed a great deal of **prosperity**.

7. REMNANTS (leftovers, pieces, fragments)
Remnants of the burnt-out missions were left behind when the new ones were built.

_____

_____

8. ENDURANCE (strength, stamina, persistence)
The Indians had a great deal of **endurance** to survive everything they did.

_____

_____

Mission Santa Clara de Asís

Answer each question below in a complete sentence.

1. Who is Mission Santa Clara de Asís named after and why was she important?

_____

_____

2. How many times was the mission destroyed by floods?

_____

_____

3. Who officiated at the dedication of Mission Santa Clara de Asís?

_____

_____

4. Why did Father Peña request military aid?

_____

_____

5. Do you think Father Peña made a wise decision? Why or why not?

_____

_____

6. What did the Jesuit Order do with the property that was deeded to them?

_____

_____

7. When were the bells damaged?

_____

_____

10. Mission San Buenventura

- March 31, 1782
- Chumash Indians
- Father Señan
- Fire, Earthquake, and Tsunami
- Water System

VOCABULARY

1. CONSTRUCTED (built, made, created)
2. DEVASTATED (shocked, upset, distraught)
3. ASYMMETRICAL (lopsided, uneven, distorted)
4. SOPHISTICATED (refined, stylish, classy)
5. FRATERNIZING (mixing, socializing, involvement)
6. ANIMOSITY (hatred, dislike, bitterness)
7. SERENE (calm, quite, still)

Mission San Buenventura

Create your own sentences below showing you understand the meaning of each vocabulary word.

1. CONSTRUCTED (built, made, created)
The churches **constructed** at the missions have survived severe weather conditions.

2. DEVASTATED (shocked, upset, distraught)
The numerous earthquakes that hit California **devastated** the missions.

3. ASYMMETRICAL (lopsided, uneven, distorted)
The design of some of the missions appear to be **asymmetrical**.

4. SOPHISTICATED (refined, stylish, classy)
As trade became more **sophisticated** at the missions, more items became available.

5. FRATERNIZING (mixing, socializing, involvement)
The priests were often found **fraternizing** with the Indians at social events.

6. ANIMOSITY (hatred, dislike, bitterness)
There were times when there was as a lot of **animosity** between the Indians and the missionaries.

7. SERENE (calm, quite, still)
The land around the missions was **serene** during the summer months.

MISSION SAN BUENVENTURA

Answer each question below in a complete sentence.

1. When construction began on the mission buildings, who came to the aid of the missionaries?

_____

_____

2. How and when was the first mission destroyed?

_____

3. Two natural disasters destroyed the newly constructed second mission and church. List them.

_____

_____

4. Do you think it was necessary for the military to be living on the grounds with the Fathers? Why or why not? Please explain your answer.

_____

_____

5. How did this mission get the water it needed to maintain all the farming that took place?

_____

_____

6. What caused tension between the fathers, the Indians, and the military?

_____

_____

7. If you were Father Señan, how would you have responded to the military's increased demands?

_____

_____

8. Why do you think Corporal Rufino Leiva imprisoned the Mojave Indians who came to see Father Señan?

_____

_____

11. Mission Santa Bárbara

- December 1, 1786
- Father Lasuén
- Chumash and Yokut
- Governor Fages
- Rebuilt Four Times
- Unique Water System
- Twin Bell Towers

VOCABULARY

1. POTENTIAL (possible, ability, capable)
2. SUSPICIOUS (doubtful, wary, doubtful)
3. DEDICATION (devotion, loyalty, allegiance)
4. INTEGRAL (important, vital, basic)
5. DEMEANOR (conduct, appearance, image)
6. INFLUENCES (persuade, promote, sway)
7. CONFISCATED (removed, seized, impounded)
8. INCEPTION (beginning, start, origin)

Create your own sentences below showing you understand the meaning of each vocabulary word.

1. POTENTIAL (possible, ability, capable)
There was a great deal of **potential** for the Indians to develop trade with the missions.

2. SUSPICIOUS (doubtful, wary, doubtful)
People not familiar with the missions often became **suspicious** about the goings-on there.

3. DEDICATION (devotion, loyalty, allegiance)
The **dedication** some Indians showed to the missions lasted a lifetime.

4. INTEGRAL (important, vital, basic)
The churches were an **integral** part of the missions for many years.

5. DEMEANOR (conduct, appearance, image)
The Indians displayed a respectful **demeanor** when they were inside the church.

6. INFLUENCES (persuade, promote, sway)
The missions were major **influences** on the structure of churches in California.

7. CONFISCATED (removed, seized, impounded)
Statues were often **confiscated** from the churches when there were invasions by intruders.

8. INCEPTION (beginning, start, origin)
At the **inception** of the missions, many of the Indians were unsure how they would be protected.

MISSION SANTA BÁRBARA

Answer each question below in a complete sentence.

1. Why didn't Governor Neve want another mission built?

___

___

2. When were the Indians and soldiers able to begin working on the construction of the barracks and other buildings for the presidio?

___

___

3. Why do you suppose Father Lasuén waited for Governor Fages before having a formal dedication for Mission Santa Bárbara?

___

___

4. How many times was the church built?

___

5. What types of materials were used in the construction of the original and the final mission?

___

___

6. Describe the unique water system.

___

___

7. What was so special about the gargoyle?

___

___

8. What does this mission have that none of the other California missions have?

___

___

51

12. Mission La Purísima Concepción

- December 8, 1787
- Chumash Indians
- Earthquake and Flooding
- Extensive Water System
- Indians Took Possession Due to Mistreatment
- California Conservation Corps

VOCABULARY

1. PROFITABLE (gainful, commercial, rewarding)
2. UNDAUNTED (fearless, carefree, unafraid)
3. ACCESSIBLE (nearby, available, open)
4. PROSPERITY (wealth, success, fortune)
5. SOPHISTICATED (classy, refined, cultured)
6. OBLIGATION (duty, requirement, commitment)
7. FORTIFICATIONS (defenses, walls, protections)
8. INCITED (prompted, encouraged, spurred)
9. SUBSERVIENT (docile, obedient, passive)

Create your own sentences below showing you understand the meaning of each vocabulary word.

1. PROFITABLE (gainful, commercial, rewarding)
The Indians often found life in the missions to be very **profitable**.

_____

_____

2. UNDAUNTED (fearless, carefree, unafraid)
Father Serra was **undaunted** after seeing how much work was left to do on the missions.

_____

_____

3. ACCESSIBLE (nearby, available, open)
The protection of the missions was **accessible** to anyone needing help.

_____

_____

4. PROSPERITY (wealth, success, fortune)
Prosperity only came to the missions after much hard work.

_____

_____

5. SOPHISTICATED (classy, refined, cultured)
The ornate designs found throughout the missions were often very **sophisticated**.

_____

_____

6. OBLIGATION (duty, requirement, commitment)
The Indians felt a true **obligation** to Father Serra.

_____

_____

7. FORTIFICATIONS (defenses, walls, protections)
Fortifications were built around some of the missions for protection.

8. INCITED (prompted, encouraged, spurred)
Attacks were often **incited** by rebels who roamed the countryside.

9. SUBSERVIENT (docile, obedient, passive)
The Indians often felt **subservient** to the priests in the missions.

MISSION LA PURÍSIMA CONCEPCIÓN

Answer each question below in a complete sentence.

1. List the groups that worked together to not only construct the mission complex, but also toiled in the fields.

2. What happened to the mission in 1812?

3. How do you think the missionaries felt when they realized so many neophytes were without food and shelter?

4. Why did the mission need warehouses?

5. How did the missionaries get water from the springs in the nearby hills to the mission?

6. Why did the Indians take possession of the mission?

7. Do you think this was a wise move for them to make? Why or why not? Explain your answer.

13. Mission Santa Cruz

- August 28, 1791
- Ohlone Indians
- Natural Resources
- Flooding and Earthquakes
- Tidal Wave
- Mrs. Gladys Sullivan Doyle

VOCABULARY

1. DESTINED (intended, meant, fated)
2. INVASION (attack, raid, conquest)
3. LUCRATIVE (profitable, worthwhile, rewarding)
4. TRESPASSING (intruding, invading, infringing)
5. PROHIBIT (forbid, bar, exclude)
6. RANSACKED (robbed, raided, vandalized)
7. DWINDLING (declining, falling, diminishing)
8. MISCELLANEOUS (mixed, jumbled, various)
9. ENVISIONED (planned, proposed, anticipated)

Create your own sentences below showing you understand the meaning of each vocabulary word.

1. DESTINED (intended, meant, fated)
All the missions built in California were **destined** to become famous.

_____

_____

2. INVASION (attack, raid, conquest)
The constant threat of **invasion** by the rebels terrified the peaceful priests.

_____

_____

3. LUCRATIVE (profitable, worthwhile, rewarding)
Foreigners often brought **lucrative** gifts to the priests at the missions.

_____

_____

4. TRESPASSING (intruding, invading, infringing)
The Fathers did not approve of the settlers **trespassing** on the mission's land.

_____

_____

5. PROHIBIT (forbid, bar, exclude)
The Spanish government tried to **prohibit** Indians from coming to the missions.

_____

_____

6. RANSACKED (robbed, raided, vandalized)
Missions were often **ransacked** and burned by the rebels.

_____

_____

7. DWINDLING (declining, falling, diminishing)
The crops began **dwindling** whenever drought hit the missions.

_____

_____

8. MISCELLANEOUS (mixed, jumbled, various)
Traders came to sell their **miscellaneous** goods and products to the missions.

_____

_____

9. ENVISIONED (planned, proposed, anticipated)
Father Serra **envisioned** a time when people could come to the missions for protection.

_____

_____

MISSION SANTA CRUZ

Answer each question below in a complete sentence.

1. Who recommended the site for Mission Santa Cruz? What river was it originally located by?

_____

_____

2. Why were the Spanish pleased with the location of the mission?

_____

_____

3. List some of the natural resources available to the mission and its residents.

_____

_____

4. What Indian tribe did this mission support?

_____

_____

5. What natural disaster caused the mission to relocate?

_____

_____

6. Why do you think the Viceroy of Mexico wanted to create a settlement so near the mission?

_____

_____

7. Do you think it was right for the settlers to steal from the mission? Why or why not?

_____

_____

8. Why did the neophytes become upset and hostile towards the Fathers?

_____

_____

14. Mission Nuestra Señora de la Soledad

- October 9, 1791
- Father Juan Crespí
- Inland Mission
- Indian Superstitions
- Archeologists
- Native Daughters of the Golden West

VOCABULARY

1. DESOLATE (deserted, barren, forsaken)
2. ISOLATION (loneliness, separation, seclusion)
3. DISCONTENT (unhappiness, sadness, displeasure)
4. PROVISIONS (supplies, rations, food)
5. RESPITE (break, relief, interval)
6. REBOUND (recovering, rallying, returning)
7. CONFISCATED (seized, stolen, impounded)
8. ABANDONED (deserted, vacant, discarded)

MISSION NUESTRA SEÑORA DE LA SOLEDAD

Create your own sentences below showing you understand the meaning of each vocabulary word.

1. DESOLATE (deserted, barren, forsaken)
Some of the missions were located in **desolate** areas of California.

_____

_____

2. ISOLATION (loneliness, separation, seclusion)
Many of the priests suffered **isolation** in the mission because they were away from their families.

_____

_____

3. DISCONTENT (unhappiness, sadness, displeasure)
At first there was a great deal of **discontent** among the Indians.

_____

_____

4. PROVISIONS (supplies, rations, food)
There were more than enough **provisions** for everyone who lived in the missions.

_____

_____

5. RESPITE (break, relief, interval)
The missions were often places of **respite** for those in need.

_____

_____

6. REBOUND (recovering, rallying, returning)
After the earthquakes, it took a while for the missions to **rebound**.

_____

_____

7. CONFISCATED (seized, stolen, impounded)
The rebels often **confiscated** statues from the church when they attacked.

_____

_____

8. ABANDONED (deserted, vacant, discarded)
Some of the Indians **abandoned** the mission after the rebels came.

_____

_____

Mission Nuestra Señora de la Soledad

Answer each question below in a complete sentence.

1. Where did the name *Soledad* come from?

2. What was different about the location of Mission Nuestra Señora de la Soledad?

3. Describe the weather in this area.

4. Why did Father Juan Crespí say the Indians were "blown in by the four winds?"

5. What happened to the Indians who lived and worked at the mission in 1802?

6. The archeologists who discovered the ruins of Mission Nuestra Señora de la Soledad were from what place?

7. What organization came to the aid of the mission and how did this organization help the mission?

15. Mission San José

- June 11, 1797
- Military Presence
- Outdoor Laundry Facility
- Estanislao
- Father Durán
- Native Daughters of the Golden West Foundation

VOCABULARY

1. UNRULY (rowdy, wild, willful)
2. IMPROVISED (created, invented, adlibbed)
3. CAMPAIGNED (ran, fought, crusaded)
4. PROCLAIMING (stating, declaring, pronouncing)
5. PARDON (forgiveness, absolution, mercy)
6. REMNANTS (scrap, leftover, pieces)
7. REPLICA (copy, model, facsimile)
8. ARTIFACTS (relics, pieces, objects)

Create your own sentences below showing you understand the meaning of each vocabulary word.

1. UNRULY (rowdy, wild, willful)
Some Indians became **unruly** when they felt threatened.

_____

_____

2. IMPROVISED (created, invented, adlibbed)
Before the churches were built, the priests had to **improvise** by holding mass outside.

_____

_____

3. CAMPAIGNED (ran, fought, crusaded)
The priests **campaigned** the Spanish government for support of their missions.

_____

_____

4. PROCLAIMING (stating, declaring, pronouncing)
Indians were **proclaiming** their faith by attending mass.

_____

_____

5. PARDON (forgiveness, absolution, mercy)
The priests were willing to **pardon** the Indians for their sins.

_____

_____

6. REMNANTS (scrap, leftover, pieces)
The Indian women would use **remnants** to make garments for the priests.

_____

_____

Mission San José

7. REPLICA (copy, model, facsimile)
A **replica** of the original bell has been placed in all the missions.

_____

_____

8. ARTIFACTS (relics, pieces, objects)
There are **artifacts** in all the missions showing what life was like.

_____

_____

Mission San José

Answer each question below in a complete sentence.

1. Mission San José could have been established for one of two reasons. List them.

_____

_____

2. Who caused most of the trouble in the area this mission was located?

_____

_____

3. List the materials used in the construction of this mission.

_____

_____

4. Why do you suppose they would ring a bell to announce the arrival of guests?

_____

_____

5. Where did they get the water for the outdoor laundry facility?

_____

_____

6. What is another name for a priest's residence building?

_____

_____

7. Why do you think Estanislao returned to Father Durán?

_____

_____

16. Mission San Juan Bautista

- June 24, 1797
- Mutsun Indians
- San Andreas Fault
- Barrel Organ
- William Randolph Hearst Foundation

VOCABULARY

1. CIVILIZE (refine, educate, develop)
2. DEMOLISHED (ruined, wrecked, damaged)
3. OPPORTUNITY (chance, occasion, break)
4. SANCTUARY (reserve, refuge, shelter)
5. SECURED (safe, available, open)
6. LOYALTY (devotion, dependability, trustworthy)
7. PROSPERITY (wealth, success, fortune)
8. SELF-SUSTAINING (supporting, filling, satisfying)
9. ASSIGNED (given, appointed, delegated)
10. FORLORN (lonely, lost, pitiful)

MISSION SAN JUAN BAUTISTA

Create your own sentences below showing you understand the meaning of each vocabulary word.

1. CIVILIZE (refine, educate, develop)
The priests tried to **civilize** the Indians who came to the missions.

_____

_____

2. DEMOLISHED (ruined, wrecked, damaged)
Some buildings at the missions were **demolished** by the earthquakes.

_____

_____

3. OPPORTUNITY (chance, occasion, break)
The mission provided the Indians with the **opportunity** to be safe from the rebels.

_____

_____

4. SANCTUARY (reserve, refuge, shelter)
The missions were a **sanctuary** for the Indians and their families.

_____

_____

5. SECURED (safe, available, open)
The safety of the missions was **secured** by the California government.

_____

_____

6. LOYALTY (devotion, dependability, trustworthy)
Loyalty was quite common between the priests and the Indians during this time period.

_____

_____

7. PROSPERITY (wealth, success, fortune)
There was a great deal of **prosperity** within the missions due to the extended trade.

8. SELF-SUSTAINING (supporting, filling, satisfying)
The missions became **self-sustaining** after the productivity of the crops was increased.

9. ASSIGNED (given, appointed, delegated)
The Spanish government **assigned** guards to the mission to control them.

10. FORLORN (lonely, lost, pitiful)
Many Indians felt **forlorn** when they learned the Spanish government was going to take control of the missions.

MISSION SAN JUAN BAUTISTA

Answer each question below in a complete sentence.

1. What geological fault is Mission San Juan Bautista built over?

___

2. Which Indian tribe aided the Fathers in the construction of this mission?

___

3. How was this mission church different from the others?

___

4. Why do you think the noise from the barrel organ frightened the Indians?

___

5. How do you think the Indians felt when they were declared "free?"

___

6. What happened in California in 1846?

___

7. Where can you find some of the original mission tiles?

___

8. What big foundation helped fund the restoration of this mission?

___

17. Mission San Miguel Arcángel

- July 25, 1797
- Father Antonio de la Concepćion Horra
- Salinas River
- William Reed
- Central Valley
- Dance Hall and Saloon

VOCABULARY

1. MEDICINAL (medical, healing, tonic)
2. INITIAL (first, primary, early)
3. TRANSPORTED (moved, brought, carried)
4. EXTERIOR (outside, surface, front)
5. VIBRANT (lively, bubbly, energetic)
6. SOPHISCATED (mature, advanced, developed)
7. TENDING (nursing, managing, supervised)
8. PRIORITY (importance, prominent, rank)
9. INTRUSION (invasion, meddling, disturbance)

Create your own sentences below showing you understand the meaning of each vocabulary word.

1. MEDICINAL (medical, healing, tonic)
The hot springs were used for **medicinal** purposes.

_____

_____

2. INITIAL (first, primary, early)
The **initial** missions were often considered a place for protection.

_____

_____

3. TRANSPORTED (moved, brought, carried)
Animals were **transported** to the missions by the Indians.

_____

_____

4. EXTERIOR (outside, surface, front)
The **exterior** mission walls were made of adobe rock.

_____

_____

5. VIBRANT (lively, bubbly, energetic)
The priests were very **vibrant** when it came to preaching the gospels.

_____

_____

6. SOPHISTICATED (mature, advanced, developed)
The workmanship in the cathedrals was **sophisticated**.

_____

_____

7. TENDING (nursing, managing, supervised)
Indians were **tending** to the crops while the priests were tending to the churches.

_____

_____

8. PRIORITY (importance, prominent, rank)
The restoration of the missions was the first **priority** of the priests.

_____

_____

9. INTRUSION (invasion, meddling, disturbance)
The **intrusion** of the rebels caused a lot of trouble in the missions.

_____

_____

MISSION SAN MIGUEL ARCÁNGEL

Answer each question below in a complete sentence.

1. When was the cross raised for Mission San Miguel Arcángel?

_____

_____

2. How did the Indians in the area react to the construction of the mission?

_____

_____

3. Why was Father Antonio de la Concepćion Horra removed from this mission?

_____

_____

4. Where did the mission get its water for farming?

_____

_____

5. Where were the Fathers looking to expand the development of missions?

_____

_____

6. Do you think it was wise of William Reed to brag to guests about his gold? Why or why not? Explain your answer.

_____

_____

7. Although part of the mission became a saloon and a dance hall, the buildings were never damaged. What kept people from damaging the mission?

_____

_____

75

18. Mission San Fernando Rey de España

- September 8, 1797
- Gold
- John C. Fremont
- Vandals
- Landmarks Club
- Bob Hope

VOCABULARY

1. DEDICATION (devotion, loyalty, allegiance)
2. PICTURESQUE (pretty, scenic, pleasing)
3. REIGN (rule, control, govern)
4. SEIZURE (attack, capture, abduction)
5. PRESERVATION (defense, salvation, protection)
6. ACCUMULATED (added, collected, gathered)

Create your own sentences below showing you understand the meaning of each vocabulary word.

1. DEDICATION (devotion, loyalty, allegiance)
The priests had complete **dedication** to the missions.

2. PICTURESQUE (pretty, scenic, pleasing)
From a distance, the missions were quite **picturesque**.

3. REIGN (rule, control, govern)
The priests tried to **reign** over the missions.

4. SEIZURE (attack, capture, abduction)
The attempted **seizure** of the missions was very distressing to the priests.

5. PRESERVATION (defense, salvation, protection)
The **preservation** of the missions was the most important thing for Father Serra.

6. ACCUMULATED (added, collected, gathered)
The priests **accumulated** great artifacts in the missions.

Mission San Fernando Rey de España

Answer each question below in a complete sentence.

1. How many baptisms took place the day of Mission San Fernando Rey de España's dedication?

2. Explain the legend surrounding this mission.

3. Why did vandals dig through the mission grounds?

4. List some of the uses of the mission when it was seized in 1847.

5. What organization supervised the preservation of this mission?

6. What famous entertainer is buried in the San Fernando Mission Cemetery?

19. Mission San Luis Rey de Francia

- June 13, 1789
- San Diego Presidio
- A Round Dome
- Military and Priests
- Father Peyri
- Pepper Tree
- Pauma Indian Reservation

VOCABULARY

1. CRUCIAL (important, necessary, decisive)
2. TEMPORARY (brief, fleeting, momentary)
3. DOME (vault, roof, ceiling)
4. ELABORATE (elegant, decorative, rich)
5. EXOTIC (unusual, different, striking)
6. FEASIBLE (possible, likely, achievable)
7. MENTOR (teacher, advisor, supporter)
8. PROSPERED (thrived, grown, flourished)
9. ENCROACHED (invaded, infringed, trespassed)
10. ILLEGAL (banned, dishonest, criminal)

Mission San Luis Rey de Francia

Create your own sentences below showing you understand the meaning of each vocabulary word.

1. CRUCIAL (important, necessary, decisive)
It was **crucial** that the priests were able to protect the Indians.

_____

_____

2. TEMPORARY (brief, fleeting, momentary)
Temporary buildings were erected before the missions were built.

_____

_____

3. DOME (vault, roof, ceiling)
It took years for the priests to build the **dome** of the cathedral.

_____

_____

4. ELABORATE (elegant, decorative, rich)
The **elaborate** design of the cathedrals brought many admirers to the missions.

_____

_____

5. EXOTIC (unusual, different, striking)
Many **exotic** travelers came to the missions.

_____

_____

6. FEASIBLE (possible, likely, achievable)
The Fathers found it **feasible** to provide protection to anyone who came.

_____

_____

7. MENTOR (teacher, advisor, supporter)
Father Serra was a **mentor** for many of the Indians.

_____

_____

8. PROSPERED (thrived, grown, flourished)
The missions **prospered** when the Indians were able to trade their goods.

_____

_____

9. ENCROACHED (invaded, infringed, trespassed)
The rebels **encroached** on the territory of the missions.

_____

_____

10. ILLEGAL (banned, dishonest, criminal)
It was **illegal** for the Spanish government to control the missions.

_____

_____

Mission San Luis Rey de Francia

Answer each question below in a complete sentence.

1. There was a group of Indians and soldiers who built the mission. Where did they come from?

2. When the new church was completed, how many people could it hold?

3. What unique element was constructed at this mission?

4. Why was it necessary to build San Antonio de Pala Asistencia?

5. How do you think Father Serra would have felt about the "sub-mission," San Antonio de Pala Asistencia?

6. Why do you think there were bad feelings between the military and the priests?

7. If you were a neophyte living at the mission, how would you have felt when you heard Father Peyri was leaving? Explain your answer.

8. Who came in and began the restoration process of this mission?

_____

_____

9. In the garden there are many rare plant specimens. Among them is a tree that is the first of its species grown in California. What is it?

_____

_____

10. Why didn't San Antonio de Pala Asistencia fall into the same destruction and disrepair as the mission?

_____

_____

20. Mission Santa Inés

- September 17, 1804
- San Rafael Mountains
- Indians Rebel
- Our Lady of Refuge of Sinners
- Tramps, Hobos, and Wayfarers
- Knights of Columbus

VOCABULARY

1. FERTILE (rich, lush, fruitful)
2. POTENTIAL (possible, likely, thinkable)
3. ABUNDANT (rich, plentiful, lavish)
4. UNDAUNTED (fearless, carefree, unconcerned)
5. DESTRUCTION (damage, ruin, demolition)
6. OPPRESSIVE (cruel, unfair, harsh)
7. BANISHED (exiled, displaced, expelled)
8. CONFISCATE (remove, seize, impound)
9. INSTITUTION (organization, society, association)

Create your own sentences below showing you understand the meaning of each vocabulary word.

1. FERTILE (rich, lush, fruitful)
The Indians worked the **fertile** land in California to help the missions.

2. POTENTIAL (possible, likely, thinkable)
The missions' **potential** was beyond anyone's belief.

3. ABUNDANT (rich, plentiful, lavish)
The crops were **abundant** enough to feed the people who lived in the missions.

4. UNDAUNTED (fearless, carefree, unconcerned)
Father Serra was **undaunted** by the attacks of the rebels on the missions.

5. DESTRUCTION (damage, ruin, demolition)
The **destruction** of buildings and property at the missions was a serious problem for the priests.

6. OPPRESSIVE (cruel, unfair, harsh)
The rebels exhibited **oppressive** behavior towards the priests and Indians.

MISSION SANTA INÉS

7. BANISHED (exiled, displaced, expelled)
Rebels who fought the priests were **banished** from the missions.

8. CONFISCATE (remove, seize, impound)
Rebels tried to **confiscate** sacred statues from the cathedrals.

9. INSTITUTION (organization, society, association)
Government **institution** caused many problems for the missions.

MISSION SANTA INÉS

Answer each question below in a complete sentence.

1. Where is this mission located?

_____

2. What happened on September 17, 1804?

_____

_____

3. What do you think the author meant when she stated the "Chumash Indian's craftsmanship with leather and metal was unparalleled?"

_____

_____

4. List the materials used in the reconstruction of the mission after it was destroyed by an earthquake.

_____

_____

5. Why did the Indians rebel?

_____

_____

6. The College of Our Lady of Refuge of Sinners had what distinction?

_____

_____

7. Some very unusual individuals were put to work during the restoration of the mission. Who were they and what were they called?

_____

_____

8. Where did some of the funds come from for the restoration of the mission?

_____

_____

21. Mission San Rafael Arcángel

- December 14, 1817
- Designed as Hospital
- Smaller than the other Missions
- Gypsies
- No Drawings/Photographs
- William Randolph Hearst Foundation

VOCABULARY

1. BENEFITED (helped, profited, aided)
2. ENCOMPASSING (surround, enclose, pull together)
3. RESEMBLE (look alike, similar, take after)
4. PRIMARILY (mostly, chiefly, mainly)
5. ADMINISTER (manage, direct, control)
6. PROSPEROUS (wealthy, affluent, successful)
7. AGGRAVATED (annoyed, forced, provoked)
8. TRANSPLANTED (moved, relocated, shifted)
9. TENDRIL (shoot, vine, stem)

Create your own sentences below showing you understand the meaning of each vocabulary word.

1. BENEFITED (helped, profited, aided)
Everyone at the missions **benefited** when they worked together.

2. ENCOMPASSING (surround, enclose, pull together)
The missions could be large, often **encompassing** a sizable area of land.

3. RESEMBLE (look alike, similar, take after)
Skilled craftsmanship made some of the cathedrals **resemble** the Vatican.

4. PRIMARILY (mostly, chiefly, mainly)
People **primarily** came to the missions to praise God.

5. ADMINISTER (manage, direct, control)
The priests had to **administer** the daily events of the missions.

6. PROSPEROUS (wealthy, affluent, successful)
Because the Indians and their families worked so hard, the farmland became **prosperous**.

7. AGGRAVATED (annoyed, forced, provoked)
The priests were **aggravated** by rebel attacks.

9. TRANSPLANTED (moved, relocated, shifted)
Many Indians felt they had been **transplanted** to the missions against their will.

10. TENDRIL (shoot, vine, stem)
The Indians were able to take **tendrils** of plants and transform them into crops for the missions.

Mission San Rafael Arcángel

Answer each question below in a complete sentence.

1. What was Mission San Rafael Arcángel originally designed to be used for?

___

___

2. Why do you think this mission was smaller than the others?

___

___

3. This mission was lacking certain things a regular mission had; list at least two of them.

___

___

4. Mission San Rafael Arcángel was home to many individuals. List some who claimed this mission their home.

___

___

5. Why was it difficult to replicate this mission during the restoration process?

___

___

6. What foundation funded the restoration of this small mission?

___

___

22. Mission San Francisco Solano de Sonoma

- July 4, 1823
- Russian Trade
- Father Altimira
- John C. Fremont
- California Republic Flag

VOCABULARY

1. **UNIQUE** (distinct, rare, one-of-a-kind)
2. **SUPPRESSION** (conquest, defeat, dominance)
3. **COMPROMISE** (settlement, arrangement, agreement)
4. **CONVERSION** (change, switch, move)
5. **THWARTING** (ruining, preventing, spoiling)
6. **GENEROUS** (lavish, kind, plentiful)
7. **FLEDGLING** (new, untried, inexperienced)
8. **THRIVED** (flourished, increased, succeeded)
9. **VANDALIZED** (destroyed, ruined, wrecked)
10. **DISPOSITION** (character, temper, mood)
11. **PERSECUTING** (bullying, tormenting, mistreating)
12. **PROCLAMATION** (announcement, edict, declaration)

Create your own sentences below showing you understand the meaning of each vocabulary word.

1. UNIQUE (distinct, rare, unusual)
Because the missions were **unique**, people came from all over to see them.

2. SUPPRESSION (conquest, defeat, dominance)
The Indians revolted due to the priests' harsh **suppression**.

3. COMPROMISE (settlement, arrangement, agreement)
It was important that there was always a fair **compromise** between the priests and the Indians.

4. CONVERSION (change, switch, move)
The religious **conversion** of some of the Indians did not always come easily.

5. THWARTING (ruining, preventing, spoiling)
Both priests and Indians worked together, **thwarting** the efforts of the rebels.

6. GENEROUS (lavish, kind, plentiful)
Visitors to the missions were often **generous** with their donations.

7. FLEDGLING (new, untried, inexperienced)
The **fledgling** missions suffered greatly early on.

8. THRIVED (flourished, increased, succeeded)
Even though the mission **thrived** because of the hard work of the Indians, nature often inflicted repeated damage to them with storms and earthquakes.

9. VANDALIZED (destroyed, ruined, wrecked)
Rebels often **vandalized** the church just to be mean and hurtful.

10. DISPOSITION (character, temper, mood)
The **dispositions** of the priests never changed because they believed in the hard work on the missions.

11. PERSECUTING (bullying, tormenting, mistreating)
When the rebels were **persecuting** the Indians, it motivated the priests to work harder to protect the success of the missions.

12. PROCLAMATION (announcement, edict, declaration)
The priests delivered their **proclamation** to the Indians after they attended mass and had been fed.

MISSION SAN FRANCISCO SOLANO DE SONOMA

Answer each question below in a complete sentence.

1. What was Mission San Francisco Solano de Sonoma named for?

_____

_____

2. This mission was founded and established under unique circumstances. Describe them.

_____

_____

3. Who did the missionaries trade with and how did the trading begin?

_____

_____

4. Given the circumstances of the treatment of the Indians, do you agree with their revolting and vandalizing the mission? Why or why not?

_____

_____

5. Why did the Indians change their attitude?

_____

_____

6. Who supported Captain John C. Fremont in taking control of Mission Sonoma and raising the California Republic flag?

_____

_____

7. What is the oldest structure in Sonoma?

_____

_____

Directed Reading Comprehension Activity

DIRECTIONS: Read a specified amount and write down key points from each section.

1. _____

_____

_____

_____

2. _____

_____

_____

_____

3. _____

_____

_____

_____

4. _____

_____

_____

_____

Venn Diagram

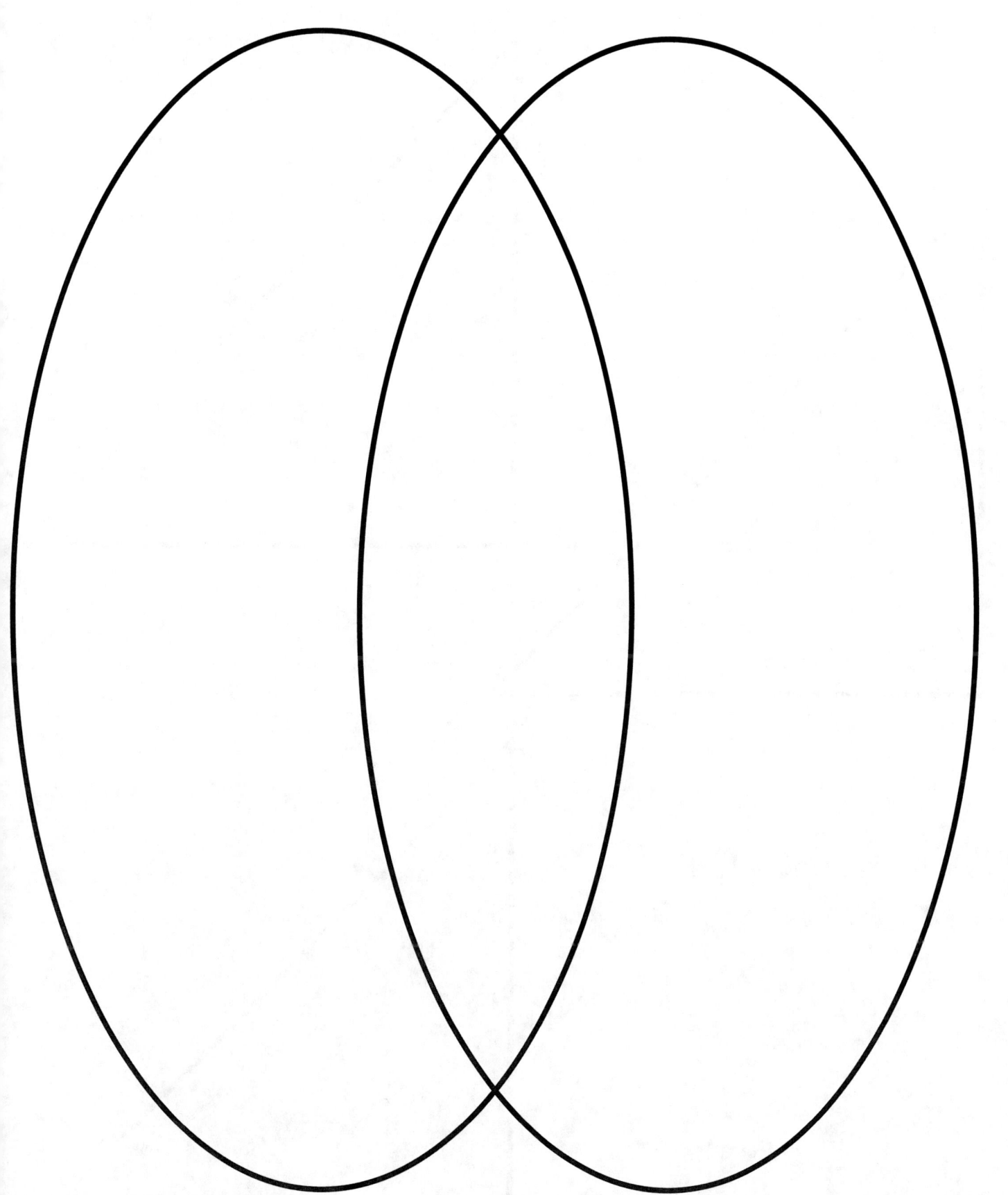

Triangle Comparison of Missions

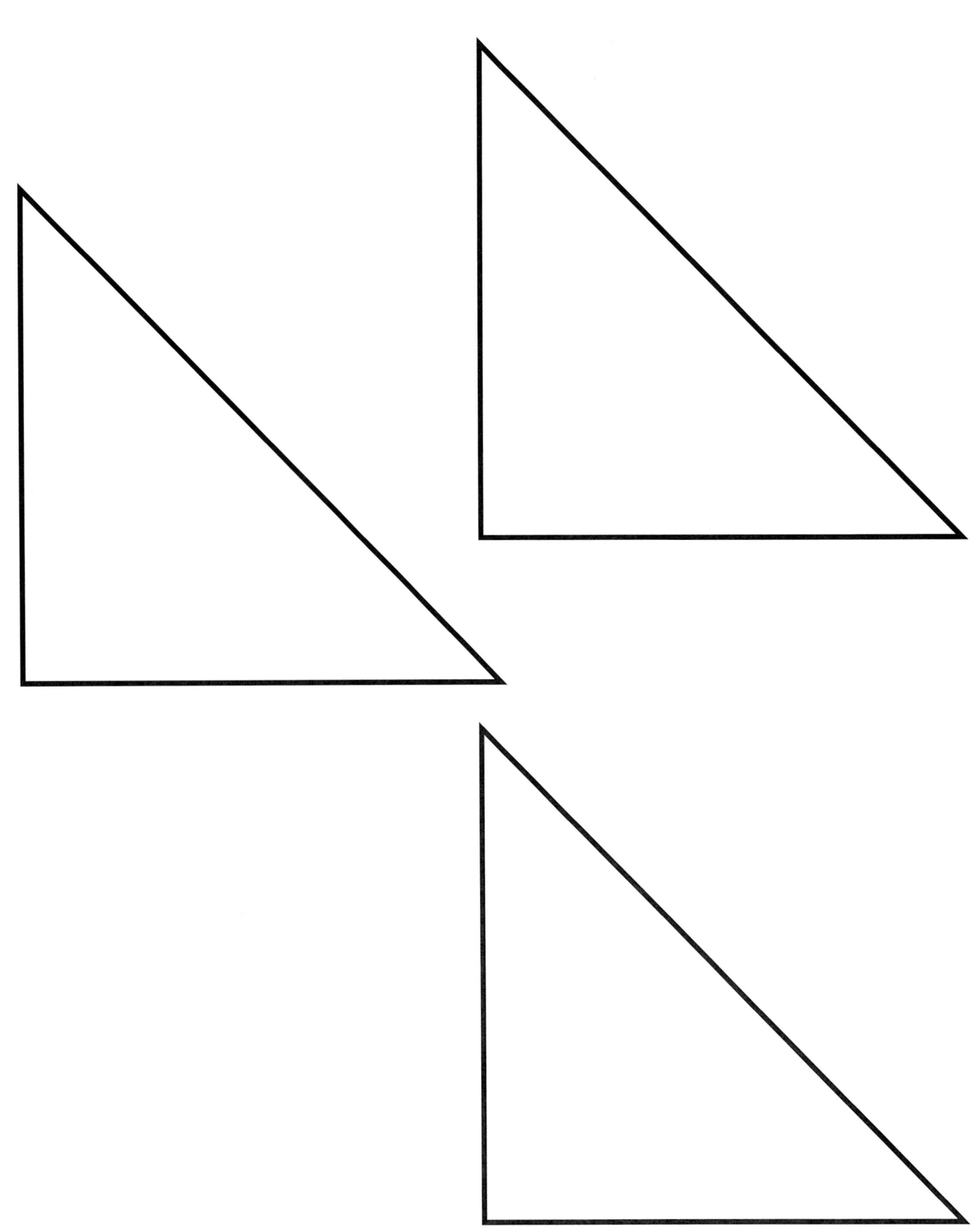

Comprehension Quiz

Teachers,

There are five categories in this game. Included are the categories, the clues and the "answers." This game is based on Pat Hunter and Janice Stevens' book, *Remembering the California Missions*. How you play the game with your class is up to you. Have fun!

Categories:

1. **Who?**

    a) He led an expedition in 1769.

    (Who was Gaspár de Portolá?)

    b) He was a notorious pirate invading many missions.

    (Who was Hypolite Bouchard?)

    c) He was appointed superior of the Baja California Missions.

    (Who was Father Junípero Serra?)

    d) He was governor of Alta California more than once.

    (Who was Pio Píco?)

    e) They were friendly, local Indians in the San Luis Obispo area.

    (Who were the Chumash Indians?)

    f) He restored the Carmel Mission.

    (Who was Harry Downie?)

2. **What?**

    a) A person sent on a religious mission.

    (What is a missionary?)

    b) This is a break in a rock formation.

    (What is a fault?)

c) A long narrow piece of land projecting into a sea or lake.

   (What is a peninsula?)

   d) A roof covering made from straw or reeds.

   (What is thatch?)

   e) To forcibly take possession of.

   (What is to seize?)

   f) Buildings that suffered much damage.

   (What are ruins?)

3. **Name That Mission!**

   a) It became a thriving trade center for the exchange of gold.

   (What is Mission San José?)

   b) It was restored with the help of tramps, hobos, and wayfarers.

   (What is Mission Santa Inés?)

   c) It has a garden sculpture of Father Serra in the cemetery.

   (What is Mission Dolores / Mission San Francisco De Asís?)

   d) It was the first mission to use red tiles on its roof.

   (What is Mission San Antonio de Padua?)

   e) This mission had the first pepper tree in California.

   (What is San Luis Rey de Francia?)

   f) This mission rests on the San Andreas Fault.

   (What is San Juan Bautista?)

4. **Where?**

   a) This country commissioned expeditions in the New World.

   (What is Spain?)

   b) Bells in a tower are located here.

   (Where is the belfry?)

c) Baptisms take place in the section.

   (Where is the baptistry?)

d) The place where a journey ends.

   (Where is the terminus?)

e) A fort where soldiers are housed.

   (Where is the presidio?)

f) The central part of a church.

   (Where is the nave?)

5. **Signs and Symbols**

   a) A square or rectangular courtyard enclosed by buildings.

   (What is a quadrangle?)

   b) A tall vertical structure used for supporting a building.

   (What is a pillar?)

   c) These were burned into trees as markers.

   (What are crosses?)

   d) Guidepost bells were set up along this route.

   (What is El Camino Reál?)

   e) A wreath of flowers.

   (What is a garland?)

   f) A liturgical garment worn by a priest.

   (What is a vestment?)

Review Questions

Name_____   Date_____

Answer each question below in a complete sentence.

1. What do you think Father Serra would say if he saw his missions today?

_____

_____

2. Which mission was called "The Jewel of the Missions?"

_____

_____

3. Which mission was called "The Queen of the Mission?"

_____

_____

4. Which mission was called "The Mission of Music?"

_____

_____

5. Which mission was called "The Mission of the Valley?"

_____

_____

6. Which mission was known by two names: "Hidden Gem of the Missions" and "Mission of the Passes?"

_____

_____

7. Which mission was called "The King of the Missions?"

_____

_____

8. What do you think would have happened to the missions if the Mexican War of Independence had not taken place?

_____

_____

9. How about the Indians who were baptized in the missions—would their lives have been different if they were not abused by soldiers?

_____

_____

10. What natural disasters caused damage to so many of the missions in California?

_____

_____

11. Who were the key presidents in returning the California missions to the Catholic Church?

_____

_____

12. Why were the U.S. Land Commission and the U.S. Court so important to the history of the missions?

_____

_____

13. Which mission has the distinction of having the only remaining example of the Neophyte family housing?

_____

_____

14. What do you think it means when someone found respite at the missions?

15. Why do you think all missions were built with thick walls?

16. Which mission contains some of the finest examples of Spanish art in America?

17. All the missions had bells. List some events for which the bells would be rung.

18. List the explorers who visited Alta California.

19. How many missions were established in Alta California?

20. What is another name for El Camino Reál?

21. Why do you think the padres burned crosses into trees and scattered mustard seed?

Mission Question Answers

Chapter 1. El Camino Reál

1. What was another name for the "El Camino Reál?" (The King's Highway)
2. How far did El Camino Reál extend? (700 miles)
3. . (crosses were burned onto trees as markers)
4. Who chose the mission bell on a walking stick to become the new permanent marker to identify the roadway for the missions? (Mrs. Armitage S. C. Forbes)
5. How was the last mission identified in 1963 marking the end of the El Camino Reál? (a plaque was placed at the San Diego Mission, which read "El Camino Reál")

Chapter 2. Mission San Diego de Alcalá

1. Which mission is considered the mother of the California missions? (Mission San Diego de Alcalá) And why do you think is was given this name? (first mission established)
2. Describe what happened to Mission San Diego de Alcalá. (The Indians attacked because they did not like the way they were being treated by the soldiers; they also felt threatened by the spiritual influence of the mission.)
3. Why were the missionaries not able to save the land (Mexico won its independence from Spain and began to occupy Alta California. The government then started selling the land.)
4. Explain why Mission San Diego de Alcalá had to be rebuilt three times. (wrong location, destruction by Indian uprising, and earthquake)

Chapter 3. Mission San Carlos Borromea de Carmelo

1. When was this mission formally established? (June 3, 1770)
2. This was another mission that had to be relocated. Why? (It lacked available drinking water and there was a shortage of Indians to be evangelized.)
3. Describe how Father Serra lived. (simply, small cell with a cot of boards and a single blanket, a table with a candlestick, a chair, a chest, and a small collection of books)
4. When did Father Serra die? (August 28, 1784)
5. Where was Father Serra's body laid to rest? (he was entombed in the large stone church in the Carmel Mission)
6. Who rescued the Mission San Carlos Borromea de Carmelo in 1931 from being totally destroyed? (Harry Downie and his associates)
7. The chapel at this mission enjoys what distinction? (the oldest stone building in California)

Chapter 4 Mission San Antonio de Padua

1. When was Mission San Antonio de Padua founded? (July 14, 1771)
2. Why do you think Father Serra felt so good about selecting this spot for a mission? (It was near a stream, and appearance of a single Indian woman made him believe more would come.)
3. Who provided the labor for the construction of the mission compound? (the Salinan Indians)
4. List some events that occurred which caused the deterioration of Mission San Antonio de Padua (change from Spanish to Mexican rule, existence of military in mission, decline of Indian population due to European diseases, seizing of mission property, Indians no longer protected by missionaries, fields left unattended, remote location led to ransackers and plunderers, the materials used to build the mission were stolen and sold, the mission was left abandoned)

Mission Question Answers

5. Why do you think Abraham Lincoln decreed the mission be returned to the hierarchy of the Catholic Church? (It originally belonged to the church and was seized through the Secularization Act)

6. Who was influential in the restoration of this mission? (Joseph R. Knowland)

7. What happened in 1906 that caused more problems with the restoration of the mission? (earthquake)

8. Why is the statue of Saint Anthony important to this mission? (Father Serra named the mission for this saint, renowned for being a miracle worker, defending the poor and his preaching)

Chapter 5. Mission San Gabriel Archángel

1. Do you believe the legend about what brought peace between the Tongva Indians and the fathers? Explain your answer.

2. What caused the goodwill that was established between the Indians and the fathers to be destroyed? (the soldiers abuse of the Indians and the assault on the chieftain's wife)

3. Mission San Gabriel Archángel was built two times. Explain why and describe the materials used to build and rebuild it. (Originally built using saplings, willows, and reed from the riverbed.) The river flooded the area and the mission was moved to higher ground. The second time it was built with adobe bricks)

4. Where did the copper baptismal font and silver baptismal shell come from? (Spain)

5. Explain why this mission was called the "Pride of all Missions." (it was rich in agriculture, wine, olive oil, farming and the hospitality shared with traders and travelers.

6. Which government confiscated the mission properties? (the Mexican government)

7. How did President James Buchanan help the mission? (he returned it to the church)

8. Why do you think it was necessary to construct the asistencia (sub-mission outpost) to Mission San Gabriel? (any reasonable answer)

9. What do you find most interesting about Joseph (Juan José) Chapman? (possibly a cohort to pirate Hypolite Bouchard, a Yankee shipbuilder, miracle worker, skilled artistry, built first gristmill, continued to aid the missionaries at the mission)

Chapter 6. Mission San Luis Obispo de Tolosa

1. Who helped the missionaries construct the original buildings and what materials did they use? (Chumash Indians, they used native materials poles, tree boughs, and other plant material)

2. Why do you think they were willing to help the missionaries? (possibly because the soldiers killed the savage bears)

3. Why did a second mission need to be constructed? (hostile Indians from the Central Valley set fires destroying the buildings)

4. List some of the items produced by this mission when it was prosperous. (wine, olive oil, fruits, vegetables, high quality cloth, and red tiles for construction of other missions)

5. Why did Father John Harnett want to tear down the modernization work done on the mission? (he wanted to restore it to its original architectural design)

6. Do you think this was a wise decision? Why or why not? (reasonable answer)

7. How was Santa Margarita Asistencia similar to Mission San Luis Obispo? (provided a mission community to feed and care for the Indians, growing crops, maintaining the granaries for storage, provide medical needs for the Indians, life was similar to that on this mission grounds)

Chapter 7. Mission San Francisco de Asis (Mission Dolores)

1. Do you think the San Francisco Bay could really accommodate all the ships in Spain? Why or why not? (reasonable answer)

2. This mission is named in honor of whom? (Saint Francis of Assisi the founder of the Franciscan order)

3. Who came to help the fathers with the construction of the mission and its buildings? (sailors from the ships such as the San Carlos)
4. What caused the Indians to flee the mission? (an epidemic of measles killed many Indians; they feared the epidemic to be evil spirits)
5. How did the Mexican War of Independence affect Mission Dolores? (began its decline, secularization took control away from the fathers, lands and possessions were confiscated, Indians abandoned the missions)
6. Describe what happened to the missions when the Gold Rush struck (high jinx, drinking, racing, gambling, part of the mission was turned into a hotel.)
7. Why do you think Mission Dolores's chapel survived an earthquake and fire when all the surrounding buildings did not? (reasonable answer)

Chapter 8. Mission San Juan Capistrano

1. What legend is celebrated every year at this mission? (the return of the swallows from Argentina)
2. Why was it necessary for Fathers de Lasuén and Amurrio to wait in San Diego before making the trip to San Juan Capistrano to set up the founding of this newest mission? (news of an Indian massacre and fear for their safety)
3. Why do you think the soldiers buried the bells? (reasonable answer)
4. What happened on November 1, 1776? (the official founding of the mission with high mass)
5. How would the missionaries benefit from teaching the Indians the skills of weaving, carpentry, and agriculture? (answers should deal with the success of the mission)
6. List the materials used in the building of the church. (heavy stones from the quarry, pebbles, small stones, limestone mortar, and sandstone)
7. Several devastating events happened to Mission San Juan Capistrano. List three of these events. (earthquakes, attacked by the pirate, Hypolite Bouchard, discontent between the military and the civil government, Mexican government came in demanding finances and products, the emancipation of the mission Indians, finally the sale of the mission to private parties)
8. What is the historical significance of the Serra Chapel? (the only chapel left where Father Serra conducted Mass, also possibly one of the oldest structures in the state)
9. Three cultures,—American Indians, Spaniards, and Mexican ranchos—are represented at the mission. Which do you think had the strongest influence and why? (reasonable answer)

Chapter 9. Mission Santa Clara de Asís

1. Who is Mission Santa Clara de Asís named after and why was she important? (Saint Claire of Assisi, the founder of the Poor Clares Order of nuns)
2. How many times was the mission destroyed by floods? (2)
3. Who officiated at the dedication of Mission Santa Clara de Asís? (Father Serra)
4. Why did Father Peña request military aid? (confrontations with the local Indians and the settlers in San Jose)
5. Do you think this was a wise decision? Why or why not? (reasonable answer)
6. What did the Jesuit Order do with the property that was deeded to them? (established Santa Clara College)
7. When were the bells damaged? (during a fire in 1926)

Chapter 10. Mission San Buenaventura

1. When construction began on the buildings for the mission, who came to the aid of the missionaries? (the Chumash Indians)
2. How and when was the first mission destroyed? (by fire in 1782)
3. Two natural disasters struck and destroyed the newly constructed second mission and church. List them (earthquake and tsunami)

MISSION QUESTION ANSWERS

4. Do you think it was necessary for the military to be living on the grounds with the fathers? Why or why not? Please explain your answer. (reasonable answer)
5. How did this mission get the water it needed to maintain all the farming that took place? (they built a reservoir and aqueduct system and a stone and mortar canal seven miles long)
6. What caused tension between the Fathers, the Indians, and the military? (no longer receiving support from Mexico and putting too many demands for food and clothing)
7. If you were Father Señan, how would you have responded to the military's increased demands? (reasonable answer)
8. Why do you think Corporal Rufino Leiva imprisoned the Mojave Indians who came to see Father Señan? (reasonable answer)

Chapter 11. Mission Santa Barbara

1. Why didn't Governor Neve want another mission built? (he was becoming suspicious of the power of the missions)
2. When were the Indians and soldiers able to begin working on the construction of the barracks and other buildings for the presidio? (when Governor Fages replaced Governor Neve)
3. Why do you suppose Father Lasuén waited for Governor Fages before having a formal dedication for Mission Santa Barbara? (possibly because he supported the construction of the mission and presidio)
4. How many times was the church built? (four times)
5. What type of material was used in the construction of the original mission and the final mission? (first was built with logs, reeds, thatch and mud the last one was built with native yellow sandstone with crushed seashells in lime mortar and red tiles for the roof)
6. Describe the unique water system. (a reservoir made of masonry, a large fountain, two stone basins and dams built on the creek, an aqueduct that carried water to the mission, some went through a filtering system for clean drinking water, and the over flow was used for laundry by the Indians)
7. What is so special about the gargoyle? (supposedly the oldest and largest Chumash Indian stone sculpture in Calif. and the gargoyle is a mountain lion)
8. What does this mission have that none of the other California missions have? (twin bell towers)

Chapter 12. Mission La Purísima Concepćion

1. List the groups that worked together to not only construct the mission complex, but also toiled in the fields. (the soldiers, Chumash Indians, and the fathers)
2. What happened to the mission in 1812? (an earthquake destroyed the mission and then it was flooded)
3. How do you think the missionaries felt with they realized so many neophytes were without food and shelter? (reasonable answer)
4. Why did the mission need warehouses? (to store soap, tallow and hides)
5. How did the missionaries get water from the springs in the nearby hills to the mission? (they created a system of aqueducts, reservoirs, and clay pipes to transport the water)
6. Why did the Indians take possession of the mission? (They were angry over the mistreatment by the soldiers)
7. Do you think this was a wise move for them to make? Why or why not? Explain your answer.

Chapter 13. Mission Santa Cruz

1. Who recommended the site for Mission Santa Cruz? What river was it originally located by? (recommended by Father Francisco Palou, it was located near the San Lorenzo River)
2. Why were the Spanish pleased with the location of the mission? (it could possibly defend the area from foreign invasion sea it also allowed easy access for ships bringing in and picking up supplies)
3. List some of the natural resources available to the mission and its residents. (fish from the sea, fresh water from the nearby river, wood from the redwood forests)

4. What Indian tribe did this mission support? (the Ohlone Indians)
5. What natural disaster caused the mission have to relocate? (flooding from the river)
6. Why do you think the viceroy of Mexico wanted to create a settlement so near the mission? (any reasonable answer i.e. Money, take power away from mission, deprive the missions of growth)
7. Do you think it was right for the settlers to steal from the mission? Why or why not? (reasonable answer)
8. Why did the neophytes become upset and hostile towards the Fathers? (they were too strict and tried to keep them from associating with the settlers)

Chapter 14. Mission Nuestra Señora de la Soledad

1. Where did the name *Soledad* come from? (the true origin tends to be a mystery but one Father Pedro Font thinks a someone in General de Portola's first expedition asked an Indian his name and this was his response)
2. What was different about where this mission was located? (it was founded in a remote desolate area instead of along the coast)
3. Describe the weather in this area. (usually cold, damp and windy)
4. Why did Father Juan Crespí say the Indians were "blown in by the four winds?" (the mission was located in a very windy location)
5. What happened to the Indians who lived and worked at the mission in 1802? (an epidemic broke out, some died from this and other fled fearing the new religion they were being taught was the reason for the deaths)
6. Where were the archeologists from who discovered the ruins of the mission? (the University of Calif. Los Angeles)
7. What organization came to the aid of the mission and how did this organization help the mission? (the Native Daughters of the Golden West came to its aid and they help restore it)

Chapter 15. Mission San José

1. Mission San José could have been established for one of two reasons. List them. (to convert the Ohlone, Yokuts Miwok, and Patwin Indians or for its military presence)
2. Who caused most of the trouble in this area? (Indian tribes)
3. List the materials used in the construction of this mission. (adobe, redwood, tile and brick)
4. Why do you suppose they would ring a bell to announce the arrival of guests? (reasonable answer)
5. Where did they get the water for the outdoor laundry facility? (from nearby hot springs)
6. What is another name for a priest's residence building? (monastery)
7. Why do you think Estanislao returned to Father Durán? (reasonable answer)

Chapter 16. Mission San Juan Bautista

1. What geological fault is Mission San Juan Bautista built over? (the San Andreas Fault)
2. Which Indian tribe aided the Fathers in the construction of this mission. (the Mutsun Indians)
3. How was this mission church different from the others? (it had a sanctuary with a central nave with two side aisles and it was also the largest church)
4. Why do you think the noise from the barrel organ frightened the Indians? (reasonable answer)
5. How do you think the Indians felt when they were declared "free?" (reasonable answer)
6. What happened in 1846? (the American flag was raised and the US military was ordered to protect the missions)
7. Where can you find some of the original tiles? (on the floor of the church)
8. What big foundation helped fund the restoration of this mission? (the William Randolph Hearst Foundation)

Chapter 17. Mission San Miguel Arcángel

1. When was the cross raised for Mission San Miguel Arcángel? (July 25, 1797)
2. How did the Indians in the area react to the construction of the mission? (the were familiar with the work of other missions and welcomed the newcomers and helped with the construction)
3. Why was Father Antonio de la Concepćion Horra removed from this mission? (because of insanity)
4. Where did the mission get its water for farming? (the Salinas River)
5. Where were the Fathers looking to expand the development of missions? (the Central Valley)
6. Do you think it was wise of William Reed to brag to guests about his gold? Why or why not? Explain your answer. (reasonable answer)
7. Although part of the mission became a saloon and dance hall, the buildings were never damaged. What kept people from damaging the mission? (the believed the church was sacred)

Chapter 18. Mission San Fernando Rey de España

1. How many baptisms took place the day of Mission San Fernando Rey de España's dedication? (forty-three)
2. Explain the legend about this mission. (the first discovery of gold in Calif. was found near the mission. The legend states shiny yellow particles were clinging to some roots from a bunch of onions.)
3. Why did vandals dig through the mission grounds? (searching for gold)
4. List some of the uses of the mission when it was seized in 1847. (a stagecoach station, a warehouse, a stable, and quarters for Colonel John C. Fremont and his army)
5. What organization supervised the preservation of this mission? (the Landmarks Club)
6. What famous entertainer is buried in the San Fernando Mission Cemetery? (Bob Hope)

Chapter 19. Mission San Luis Rey de Francia

1. There were a group of Indians and soldiers who built the mission. Where did they come from? (the San Diego Presidio)
2. When the new church was completed how many people could it hold? (1,000 people)
3. What unique element was constructed at this mission? (a round dome)
4. Why was it necessary to build San Antonio de Pala Asistencia? (to manage the growth and meet the needs of the more than 1,500 neophytes who now lived in the original mission)
5. How do you think Father Serra would have felt about the "sub-mission," San Antonio de Pala Asistencia? (reasonable answer, possibly proud or happy because something he has dreamed of)
6. Why do you think there were bad feelings between the military and the priests? (soldiers encroaching on land? Taking food? Reasonable answers)
7. If you were a neophyte living at the mission, how would you have felt when you heard Father Peyri was leaving? Explain your answer. (reasonable answer)
8. Who came in and began the restoration process of this mission? (the seminarians from the Franciscan Seminary)
9. In the garden there are many rare specimens. Among them is a tree that is the first of its species grown in California. What is it? (the pepper tree)
10. Why didn't San Antonio de Pala Asistencia fall into the same destruction and disrepair as the mission? (reasonable answers could include too far inland, on the Pauma Indian Reservation)

Chapter 20. Mission Santa Inés

1. Where is this mission located? (in the Santa Ynez Valley, between the Santa Inés and San Rafael Mountains)
2. What happened on September 17, 1804? (the cross was raised and blessed by Father Estevan Tapis)

Mission Question Answers

3. What do you think the author meant when she stated the "Chumash Indian's craftsmanship with leather and metal was unparalleled?" (reasonable answer should be positive meaning they were very talented)
4. List the materials used in the reconstruction of the mission after it was destroyed by an earthquake. (adobe, tile roof, oak, sycamore, pine, rawhide, and brick tiles on the floor)
5. Why did the Indians rebel? (they resented providing their labor to support the military)
6. The College of Our Lady of Refuge of Sinners had what distinction? (the first seminary and institution of higher learning in California)
7. Some very unusual individuals were put to work during the restoration of the mission. Who were they and what were they called? (tramps, hobos and wayfarers, they were fed and housed also, they were called "Dick Turpins")
8. Where did some of the funds come from for the restoration of the mission? (Knights of Columbus of Los Angeles and William Randoph Hearst Foundation)

Chapter 21. Mission San Rafael Arcángel

1. What was Mission San Rafael Arcángel originally designed to be used for? (to care and supply hospitalization for the neophytes who had taken ill with white men's diseases.)
2. Why do you think this mission was smaller than the others? (reasonable answer-was supposed to be a sub-mission, or a sanitarium)
3. This mission was lacking certain things a regular mission had, list at least two. (no accommodations for Indians, no bell tower, lacked a quadrangle, no granaries or warehouses)
4. Mission San Rafael Arcángel was home to many. How many do you remember? (Priests, Indians, Captain John C. Fremont, and gypsies)
5. Why was it difficult to replicate this mission during the restoration process? (no drawings or photographs remain in existence)
6. What foundation funded the restoration of this small mission? (the William Randolph Hearst Foundation)

Chapter 22. Mission San Francisco Solano de Sonoma

1. Who was Mission San Francisco Solano de Sonoma named for? (Saint Francis Solano, a Peruvian missionary)
2. This mission was founded and established under unique circumstances. Describe them. (it was founded under Mexican rule and without the authorization of the President of the California Missions)
3. Who did the missionaries trade with and how did the trading begin? (they traded with the Russians because the Russians contributed linens, utensils and bells to the mission)
4. Given the circumstances of the treatment of the Indians, do you agree with their revolting and vandalizing the mission? Why or why not? (reasonable answer-they were treated poorly by Father Altimira)
5. Why did the Indians change their attitude? (Father Altimira fled and Father Buenaventura Fortuny took over and he was a kinder person)
6. Who supported Captain John C. Fremont in taking control of Mission Sonoma and raising the California Republic flag? (American settlers who wanted to form a republic independent from Mexico)
7. What is the oldest structure in Sonoma? (the original padres' quarters)

Mission Overall - Review Questions

1. What do you think Father Serra would say if he saw his missions today? (reasonable answer)
2. Which mission was called "The Jewel of the Missions?" (San Juan Capistrano)
3. Which mission was called "The Queen of the Missions?" (Mission Santa Bárbara)
4. Which mission was called "The Mission of Music?" (Mission San Juan Bautista)
5. Which mission was called "The Mission of the Valley?" (Mission San Fernando Rey de España)

Mission Question Answers

6. Which mission was known by two names "Hidden Gem of the Missions" and "Mission of the Passes?" (Mission Santa Inés)
7. Which mission was called "The King of the Missions?" (Mission San Luis Rey de Francia)
8. What do you think would have happened to the missions if the Mexican War of Independence had not taken place? (reasonable answer)
9. How about the Indians, who were baptized in the missions, would their life have been different if they were not abused by soldiers? (reasonable answer)
10. What natural disasters caused damage to so many of the missions in California? (earthquakes and floods)
11. Who were the key presidents in returning the California missions to the Catholic Church? (Lincoln and Buchanan)
12. Why were the U. S. Land Commission and the U. S. Court so important to the history of the missions? (These two bodies saved the missions and returned them to the possession of the Catholic Church)
13. Which mission has the distinction of having the only remaining example of the Neophyte family housing? (the Mission Santa Cruz)
14. What do you think it means when someone found respite at the missions? (a place to rest and regain strength)
15. Why do you think all the missions were built with thick walls? (reasonable answer)
16. Which mission contains some of the finest examples of Spanish art in America? (Mission San Miguel Arcángel)
17. All of the missions had bells. List some events when the bells would be rung. (to announce prayer, toll for the deceased, celebrate marriages, signal the announcement of a padre or warn of danger)
18. Lists the explorers who visited Alta California (Juan Rodriguez Cabrillo, Sebastian Vizcaino, Gaspar de Portola)
19. How many missions were established in Alta California? (21)
20. What is another name for El Camino Reál? (The King's Highway)
21. Why do you think the padres burned crosses into trees and scattered mustard seed? (to mark a trail)